SOME

M000166352

somewhere

in

between

KELLY PEACOCK

**THOUGHT
CATALOG**
Books

THOUGHTCATALOG.COM
NEW YORK · LOS ANGELES

THOUGHT CATALOG Books

Copyright © 2022 Kelly Peacock.
All rights reserved.

Published by Thought Catalog Books, an imprint of the digital magazine Thought Catalog, which is owned and operated by The Thought & Expression Company LLC, an independent media organization based in Brooklyn, New York and Los Angeles, California.

This book was produced by Chris Lavergne and Noelle Beams with art direction and design by KJ Parish. Special thanks to Bianca Sparacino for creative editorial direction and Isidoros Karamitopoulos for circulation management.

Visit us at *thoughtcatalog.com* and *shopcatalog.com*.

Made in the United States of America.

ISBN 978-1-949759-47-1

This is for the ones who are somewhere in between their heartache and healing.

how easy it was for us
to avoid it, the heat
between us.

how often i think of us,
the way i looked at him
and the way he looked at me,
just the same.

the heat between us

There's something about the summertime and the blue skies above a gray city that reminds me of the days we spent at coffee shops in our shorts and tees, accidentally kicking each other's shins under the table, looking at each other for a moment too long.

How easy it was for us to avoid it, the heat between us. How often I think of us, the way I looked at him and the way he looked at me, just the same.

midsommar

You let the mosquitoes get close and eat you alive
simply because you want to feel something
other than what you've been feeling:
the ache of a love affair that never really was,
the slow burn of watching twin flames disintegrate,
the death of two people who ended up together
because the universe made it so.
You grieve the love like a loss,
as if you have no other choice,
as if two people who were together in another life
weren't together in this one
because that's just the way things go sometimes.
There's something about the humidity,
how it reminds you of his palms and
how they felt touching yours.
There's a softness to the way the
moths flutter around the light.
If someone were to ask,
Did he feel like home to you?
you might let the quiet do the talking.

I want to say something
about the bridge I'm getting over,
the tragic love affair we endured.
Maybe it was partially my fault:
all the thinking and loving and longing I did.
I sat with the hurt as if I had no other choice.
I ignored the inevitable, the obvious.
I put my faith in someone too weak to
hold my heart in their hands.

I want to hear you say that you think of me.
Even if it's a lie,
even if nothing comes from it.
All I want is to know that I mattered to you
more than you made me think I did.

to love

I want him to find it easy to love me
but I'm afraid
I might not be easy to love after all.

Memorize his body
and leave the rest
be.
Notice the sunlight,
the cracked glass.

notice the sunlight

He tells you he loves you *but not in that way*
and it feels like the sound of glass shattering.
You will want to piece it together
even though it hurts
but it doesn't matter—at least it's together.
Memorize his body and leave the rest be.
Notice the sunlight, the cracked glass.

You're the kind of person who loves hard, aren't you?

You crave love so deeply, so furiously.

You give so much of yourself to others and sometimes you neglect your own needs.

If that is your truth, so be it. But please, don't let yourself fall for the bad ones. The ones who convince you that you are anything less than significant. Don't let yourself get attached to the ones who only want to pull away. The ones with a heart that does not match your capacity to love. The ones who—you won't admit—you make excuses for.

These people are not distant because they're afraid of getting hurt, they're distant from a lack of trying. They don't fear attachment because they fear they could lose you, but because they are uncomfortable with someone seeing them for who they are, deep down.

These people give reasons for why they can't love you, and those are excuses. And that's okay. Sometimes there are souls that aren't meant to be yours to love.

So please, stop manipulating your thinking when it comes to them. Understand that if someone wants to be with you, they will be. There will be no lackluster love, excuses, mistakes.

If someone wants you—your mind, your soul, your heart— they will show you how badly they do. They will make an effort. They will prove themselves in a subtle, beautiful way. They will show you that, despite any fears they might have deep down, they want to be a part of your life, one way or another, and they will make sure it happens.

pull

Maybe we don't end up together,
I think,
and then you kiss me again.
You call it unraveling,
I call it falling apart.

You grieve the love like
a loss, as if you have
no other choice, as if two
people
who were
together
in
another
life
weren't
together
in this
one
because
that's
just
the way things go sometimes.

lust

I wish I could make him stay just by asking.
My voice is not on a loop in his head
like my legs are
around his shoulders.
He cannot hear me—
the lust clogs like wax.

I never realized it until I met him:
how trying to be friends with someone you used to love
is a lot like pulling teeth.
There is nothing easy or soft about it.

bodies are just bodies

Our fingers are distant
but our palms are open.
I have a hard time believing
his body is still skin and bones,
like it should be
in the beginning of things.
I mean, a missing rib would hurt less;
I mean, maybe not everyone believes that
bodies are just bodies.
I mean, I could drown in his throat;
I know he would let me.

It is such a beautiful feeling, isn't it?
Realizing you no longer miss them
as much as you used to love them.

The distance between
us feels thick.

Suddenly,
there's something wrong
with body heat and the
urge for something more.

it feels good until it doesn't

We are touching and talking
and it feels good until it doesn't.
The distance between us feels thick.
Suddenly there's something wrong
with body heat and the urge for something more.
Again,
it feels good until it doesn't
and I'm not sure what that means for us
except maybe
this is all I get from you
and I'm just supposed to accept it.
My fingers shake, reaching for you.
My voice is strung out.
Loving you is a lot harder than not—

place like home

When he said he did not love me,
I told him I never did either.
His voice: broken wind chimes.
His touch: kissing a stovetop before going up in flames.
In retrospect,
there was a persistent echo coming in from the bedroom.
There is no place like home.

the longing, the begging

I don't like to be spoon-fed love,
with the longing, the begging,
the chasing of affection,
the hoping for insight,
the wondering,
Is this something I really want?
Is this even worth it?

ghost

The ghost is sitting there,
heavy,
on the edge of the mattress,
his body shifting with his eyes,
his palms closing but close
to me, my uncoiled fingers, reaching.
He touches me.
Déjà vu: he loves me—
hardly—

devour

There will be nights when all you can think about are his fingers and how he treated you like a peach. Call it what you want, but the space between you and him was nothing more than just space. Your becoming only happens when he leaves you. I'm only saying this because I've been there before, I've felt disappointment in the pit of me, heavy and unmoving. I know this feeling all too well, so trust me when I tell you: don't rip open your chest and offer a piece of you for him to taste. Wait for the person who wants to devour you.

fine line

It's all about having sex and feeling sad,
he says, and I think about you.
I know there are things I can't change
but I've been praying ever since we parted,
hoping something good can come from this.

love him dirty

He has me in his palms
like a piece of forbidden fruit.
I see the demons,
the way they choke him in his sleep.
He says, *don't try to save me,*
and so I trust him the only way I know how.
I know I can love him dirty, if he lets me.
The dead roses can still grow if they let themselves.

If I mattered to you,
I wouldn't have to keep asking if I do.

I once heard that
love makes a light
sound, and so when he
hums, I listen.

when he hums

I once heard that love makes a light
sound, so when he hums, I listen.

from a hand to a body

The crosswalk light flickers
from a hand to a body,
and I look at him.
A car alarm sounds, you flinch
and your fingers curl and latch around mine.
You look at the noise.
You tighten your grip around my fingers.
I look at us,
the way I let you want me
only when I am here with you.
I squeeze your hand.
Your fingers move.
The light changes, becomes a hand.

relapsing

Wiping his bloody nose on the bed sheets and slipping under his sheets, he is asking me to leave him. *I'm no good for you. You deserve better,* he tells me. I tell him, *I know.* Lord only knows why his throat burns, why the wine turns back to water, why the water turns back to wine, back to water.

Our mouths are agape, begging
and touching in between sentences.
your palms open for me to hold
and this feels like a religion,

a faith
in
something.
We are
together
like a
book of
prayers
and our
bodies
feel like
synonyms

for love, lust, or whatever is left.

what is left

Our mouths are agape,
begging and touching
in between sentences.
Your palms open for me to hold
and this feels like a religion,
a faith in something.
We are together like a book of prayers
and our bodies feel like synonyms
for love, lust, or what is left.

the thing is

I like to think about the good things,
like his neighborhood and their brownstones,
the tree outside his living room window,
the curve of his spine,
the tenderness of his fingers twitching
as he's falling asleep,
the delicacy of the freckles on his cheeks.
But I have a hard time acknowledging
the things that matter more:
those long silences,
the heavy conversations we avoided having
because we knew they would be heavy,
the tension we never thought
would be hanging over our heads,
even after all this time.

metaphor

The reality is,
he's not mine to love
and I'm not his to try and love
anymore.
I make his body into a metaphor
because it forces me to feel it
as it's leaving.

if we see each other again

I want to know what you think about
how it ended between us,
if you blame yourself,
or fate and her clumsiness,
where home is for you,
how you feel when you're alone,
where your hands are,
if you still think of me.

unrequited

I think about the unrequited desire and the dirty lust as a means of understanding that sometimes, love isn't meant to happen between two people. As badly as you believe in what could be, it's the longing that keeps you apart.

something to settle for

I mean, I do love you, he admits,
with the blood rushing to his head
as if he were hanging upside down on a mattress.
Is this it? Is this something to settle for?
Oh—
there is a climax in his voice.
I forget the rest.

the answers

What if we don't ruin each other this time?
What happens if our hands keep meeting?

We know the answers;
we cannot keep asking ourselves this.

his

Let his name sit on your tongue.
Keep it to yourself,
swallow it.

this is how you will remember me

We split a bottle of wine
the first night we spent together.
I don't know who I was then,
besides a body of warmth,
a woman letting herself be touched by a man
with no intention of keeping me close.
I wonder if you remember this.
It was desire,
wanting within reach.
I was someone who filled a void,
who made you feel things you refused to feel.
But I see it clearly, now that you're gone:
I am warmth, a body of want,
a woman to be desired,
with a force stronger than you will ever be.
I am someone who wants to love and be loved,
and this is how you will remember me.

each time you fall in love

Like Cigarettes After Sex—"Each Time You Fall In Love"—the air between us is heavy. We deny each other our bodies and how they should be together: my lips to your neck, your chest heaving, and waiting. I want a reason to stay, to savor this space. To have the courage to speak, but knowing how easy it is, still, to choke on something, to feel my lungs surrender.

I believe in lightworkers.

I believe in gut feelings, guardian angels, spirit guides—whatever you call them, I believe there is something greater and more powerful than us, moving things around in our favor and connecting us to other souls in this Universe through a chain of light. I believe there is a powerful feeling that guides us to the people we are meant to meet in this life. We cross paths with people who are meant to change our lives in some way.

Some of these people we meet are lessons and we see that clearly. Some of these people are blessings and we see that, too. And there are some people who are blessings in disguise, someone to teach us a lesson we didn't know we needed to learn.

Sometimes these people make us shrink. Sometimes they inspire us to grow, to heal, to love. Some people we meet in this life are meant to ignite something in us and change us for the better, even if it takes a little bit of time to get there.

I believe these people are our soulmates.

I believe there are certain people we meet in this life and feel tethered to them in a way that can't be explained or denied. There is a certain ethereal feeling in our gut, believing we were meant to know them and love them—and maybe we are.

Whether these people are friends, family, lovers, people we cross paths with for a brief period of time, there are people we are meant to know for either a short time or forever. They come into our lives and change the way we look at everything, the way we feel about love, lust, and human connection. We are meant to see them and know them, for reasons we might not fully understand.

"here, be here."

I could write to you
and pretend it doesn't hurt,
or I could start a fire on the concrete between us.
With a reflecting light and a magnifying glass,
I could send a smoke signal.
If I could,
I would hope you'd see it and come running.

empty

I emptied myself
and his hands cupped and waited
for me
to drip like a leaky faucet.

For reasons we can't explain, we meet people and know we were meant to love them, even if it's just for a little while. Whether or not we stay with these people, though, a part of us will always be tethered to them, no matter how hard we try to stay apart.

soulmates

For reasons we can't explain, we meet people and know we were meant to love them, even if it's just for a little while. Whether or not we stay with these people, though, a part of us will always be tethered to them, no matter how hard we try to stay apart.

matches and a matchbox

We are in his bed
when we set our bodies on fire
and watch them lose shape.
We are made down.
Please, I beg.
Pull the nails out of the hinges.
Open. For me
to nourish the hard wood with my mouth
would be
like loving someone who lets me.
I hope he notices
how I want us to be
matches and a matchbox.
Body heat and the knack of wanting more.

something about this feels like closure

I am lonely,
he breathes into my neck
and my skin sucks it up like it is good for me.
I know, but—
before I could finish,
I let him melt into me.
I mold his body into a shape to fit with mine
because at this moment, it feels right,
like this is where we are supposed to be.
But he knows too much of me and
I don't know his secrets
the way I know his flawed, naked body.
He comes halfway and leaves just the same.
He becomes shapeless in my mind
the way all past lovers do after they've had enough of me.
Something about this feels like closure.

Our togetherness was poetic and dirty,
but for me,
that was more than enough.

our togetherness was
poetic and dirty, but
for me, that was more
than enough.

even the lovers

When you start to get close to someone,
you can feel it—
you recognize that feeling of fear
that comes out of nowhere.
It grows inside of you and, at the same time,
rots like a trauma.
It's an old memory, deep-rooted,
and for whatever reason, you push the people away.
You keep them at a distance,
even if you believe you could love them—
even if you do love them.
Even the lovers are skeptical sometimes.
Even the lovers sit on the floor of the bath-
room, crying and whimpering,
there's nothing beautiful about self-sabotage.
Maybe we keep certain people at a distance
because we know, deep in our souls,
they aren't the one for us.
Or maybe we keep people at a distance
because we know it'll hurt a lot less when they leave.
Maybe it's the universe's doing—
her subtle way of reminding us
the things we want might not be the things we need.
Maybe it's just one of life's cruel iro-
nies and we just have to live with it.

maybe it's the
Universe's doing —

her subtle way
of reminding us
that the things we want
might not be the
things we need.

gluttony

Just by you dreaming it,
I am in the kitchen, naked and pretty.
Your hands find comfort around my waist
and I pull you closer.
It's your fingers,
their movement on my skin
like feeling peach fuzz for the first time.
Our mouths open wide.
You're no good for me, I want to tell him,
but then everything becomes quiet and warm.

the nature of anxiety

For him to truly love me, I have to guide him to the pit of myself to find the root of it all: the anxiety, bending and blooming inside my guts, like vines with the flowers. I never thought about the fear of showing this side of me, how sometimes, I feel like I'm falling into quicksand and if someone gets too close, they might fall too.

pretend

It was unlike anything I've ever seen before:
The openness between us,
the sound of your voice saying my name,
the feeling of lust and love
and how I had a hard time telling the difference.
It was the way you pretended to love me,
wouldn't you agree?

unraveling

I know this will hurt:
our inevitable ending.
We have pulled our threads too much
and it's all unraveling in front of us.
If we keep pulling,
it will stop eventually.
Not on its own—
but maybe.

Losing him was just as sad as loving him.

releasing

I commit to memory the movement of his hands,
cracking and releasing.
How sure of himself he was.
How quickly my throat tightened.
I'm sorry,
I hope you understand.
My palms open.
There is nothing left for us to hold onto.

how quickly we lost
each other in the
noise.

noise

You're going to think about what else is out there,
but all of that noise is just noise, he tells me,
and a part of me believes him.
But then someone tells me,
you can't lose something you never had,
and I see it clearly now, how quickly we lost each other
in the noise.

I will admit—

I don't remember what your voice sounds like anymore,
but I do know I wish I did.

the story of us

Even after all this time—
even after I no longer have a name for it—
the story of us sticks in my memory,
like papier-mâché.
Maybe this is a good thing,
maybe this is my subconscious urging me
to use him as a muse:
Just like he used me.

without him

There will be those moments, after you part ways, that will remind you of it all—how you mistook love for adoration, for curiosity, for longing. You will see his face or hear his voice and remember how easy it was for you to get lost in it, how easy it was for you to let yourself love him, as if that was all you could do. You will recognize the feelings you denied yourself once before, how you gave so much of yourself to someone who wouldn't think twice to do the same to you.

When this happens, just sit with it. Realize who and where you are now and notice how different and beautiful your life is without him. Remind yourself how loved you are without him. Notice how hard it was at first to let him go, but how easy it is now to do it all again.

sins

No one really tells you
how often you will think of his face,
even long after it happens.
His hands and the tightness of his fingers
curling around your trembling thighs.
Your dry mouth and your closing throat.
How, years later, whenever someone touches you,
a part of you believes it's the Devil again,
finding a dirty way to devour you.

No one really tells you how hard it is
to cry in the middle of sex
because you're afraid,
because you can't stop thinking about him
and how, somewhere, he's still crawling around
and looking for someone new to touch.

No one really tells you what it's like
to look in the mirror and see your body as a cathedral.
You want to be good and holy and open.
You want to think that rosary beads do work,
that gut feelings are guardian angels,
that maybe if you wait long enough
and pray a little bit harder,
someone will finally get punished for their sins.

suffocating

I want to tell him I love him,
but instead, I only hold him close.
He kisses my forehead.
He opens his mouth to speak,
but bites his tongue instead.
I can almost see the contradictions sit-
ting at the back of his throat.
I want to ask,
it's nearly suffocating, isn't it?
but I keep the thought to myself.

to be close

I think about it a lot,
how you told me you did not believe in love,
and yet, always found a reason to be close to me.

gas light

I think I love you, I say,
and he turns on the gas light.
He makes me think of it all differently.
The polaroid of my naked body he used as a bookmark,
what he used to keep his place.
Our slow dancing in the kitchen
was because of the music,
not because he wanted to keep me close.
I see it clearly now.
I look at the ceiling light above the stove
and wonder if it feels burnt out too.

sometimes the love you
want might not be meant
for you, and what you
deserve is so much greater
and is out there waiting
for you.

a means of moving on

If they give you a million reasons
why you should walk away
and they leave before you can,
commit to memory their movements.
Use them as a means of moving on.
Understand that
sometimes the love you want
might not be meant for you,
and what you deserve is so much greater
and is out there waiting for you.

the burden

I cannot handle the burden of loving
and not being loved in return,
and somehow,
I let him convince me to look at caring as a weakness.

this is not love, but longing

It feels like a slow burn, watching a candle empty of its wax with the flame flickering out, hoping it would stay a little longer. It's the thinking that maybe there are things he wanted to tell me but never had the courage to say. It's the hope that our story has a cliffhanger, even though it doesn't.

empathy

I care too much
about everyone and everything
and I have a hard time forgiving myself for it.

love language

I remind myself to look at my body
just before his leaving,
to note my movements
like the corners of pages:
my folded hands,
trembling lips desperate
to be more than just open.
This is when I learn how to want,
how to write about love
as if I understand the language
like the meaning of his body.
I put myself here
because I want to.
I feel it all;
I have to.

I remind myself to look at my body just before his leaving, to note my movements like the corner of pages: my folded hands, trembling lips desperate to ~~be~~ more than just open. This is when I learn how to want, how to write about love as if I understand the language like the meaning of his body.

I put myself here ~~because~~ I want to. I feel it all; I ~~have~~ to.

crave / fear

When your body is taken advantage of,
it becomes something you think about
for a long time after.
You look at sex as a burden
but you still pray
for those moments of intimacy.
You crave togetherness
just as much as you fear it.

tenderness

When I loved him
and when he left me—
the tenderness is the same.

there is nothing poetic about this one

You are wearing rose-colored glasses
and ripping your heart out of your chest
like a flower from its roots
for someone who does not deserve it,
for someone who does not see what you see,
for someone who would not do the same for you.

You romanticize moments
and people
and the moments you share with those people—
and that's okay, that's the beauty of love—
but please,
don't let yourself get lost in translation
and blinded by something that does not exist.
Love can be beautiful and wild
just as it can be dirty and something to grieve.

So please,
if someone does not see the beauty your soul is,
let your eyes see what's real and in front of you
and remind yourself:
there is nothing poetic about this one.

him

"I'm sick of losing soulmates," I hear someone say,
and I can't help but think of him.

half empty

I always thought
it was about what you said
just before you let them go.
I love you and you hurt me.
I'm sorry I can't do this.
Maybe the cup is half empty right now.
Maybe you don't miss me,
though I would like to think you do.
Sooner or later, things will be different
and I'll believe
you leaving was more than just something I let happen.
I've been told that a thing will go away
once it has served its purpose.
I wonder if you think about me
as often as you think about begging for forgiveness.

Maybe you don't miss me,
though I would like to
think you do.

I wonder if you think about me
as often as you think about
begging for forgiveness.

did I mean something to you?

We ended with quiet dialogue.
It was a distant thing:
a feeling we held on to,
knowing we didn't have anything left to say,
or anything that mattered enough to say, at least.
The nights are louder with you gone.
Did I mean something to you?
I hear crickets.
Anything?

waiting for

He leaves and you're alone again.
Unsure where to go from here,
you find yourself simply waiting for him to come back.

I'll never tell you, but
I still think about you.

I always do.

I'll never tell you

I still think about you.
I always do.

suffocation

Suffocation means to love hands but to fear
hands, to see life as a body game.

quiet

Are you in love with her?
Someone asks him and he is quiet.
I'm afraid to say that
this is the answer I need.

Maybe I need to
forgive myself for
holding on too long,
for thinking you
were ~~someone~~ worth
longing for.

haunting

I know it was complicated.
We let each other go because we had to—
or else one of us would suffocate—
but I don't know why there is still a part of you in me.
Like a haunting, a shadow
standing in the corner of my room.
Maybe this is a ghostly testament
to what was lost and buried.
Maybe I need to forgive myself
for holding on too long,
for thinking you were someone worth longing for.

**there is more waiting for me
and I will love again**

And so it goes:
you love someone and then you don't anymore.
This is it, you think, *this is all there is.*
But you have to believe in something greater.
You have to believe
there is more waiting for you and you will love again.
And until that happens, be still.
Tell yourself this until it sinks in:
there is more waiting for me and I will love again.

"there is more waiting for me and I will love again."

still

Sit still, he says,
after I ask him—
for the second time—
to stop touching me.
I press my palms against his chest
as he hangs over my body
like a stench hangs over a corpse
and I can only imagine a peaceful death after this.
My body is becoming
merely flesh and bone.
I shrink.

relentless

You are a relentless fuck,
if you want me
to be honest.
I like to think of how it is over,
how there is something pitiful
about the way you made love,
not knowing the difference between touching and feeling.
Between you and me,
it was desperation.

antidepressants

I want to tell them about the lump in my throat, the heaviness of my heaving chest, the ache in my head from thinking about things too much. I am tired of grasping at the pillbox, holding the little pink pill in the palm of my hands and letting it get to me the way it was meant to. The hardest pill to swallow is the pill itself.

please

My courage sat silently between my teeth,
waiting
to not be swallowed.
Please, don't touch me there.

my body, something holy

Is he the one that got away?
My mother asks me,
after I tell her about his move to Los Angeles.
I think about his lonely arms
out there, stretched and wait-
ing for something unexpected
to seduce him
into a familiar and forbidden high.
I wonder if he feels dirty again,
like picking raw fruit from its stem
and eating it right then and there.
He pops a cherry into his mouth
and it can't see how easy it is for him
to make them wither and drip on his tongue.
I wonder if he ever wears the rosary beads—
the ones his mom gave him—
or if they're buried in the night-
stand, next to the condoms.
I wonder if his fingers touch their shape
the way he would with me,
if he ever thought of my body as something holy.

the way I look at my healing

Healing is accepting every part of you,
my therapist tells me,
and so I stand in front of the mirror and stare at myself
until something changes—
the way I look at my healing,
seeing my body as more than just a vessel
for the trauma.

When it comes to love, your body cannot survive on being an afterthought.

apology for self-abandonment

I need you to forgive yourself for it all:
how you put energy into loving someone else—
someone more than yourself—
how you were concerned about how they felt with you,
how you apologized just for exist-
ing in the same space as them,
how you begged, on your knees,
for love, as a means of keeping the peace,
how you never took a moment to think,
Am I loving myself enough?
If this is your truth, forgive yourself.
Look for closure.
Understand that you can be fascinated by someone else
and you can lay yourself bare to them
if you so please,
but it's so much more important to give
some of that magic to yourself.
When it comes to love,
your body cannot survive on being an afterthought.

There are parts of me that are still
healing and that is okay.
I will be okay.

Your anger and shame are asking something of you, my therapist tells me and all I can do is cry. A heaving chest with silent, hopeless sobs—this is how I respond to it, this is all I can get myself to do. Shining a light on my shame and anger is not something I want to do, it's nothing I want to think about, even though I know I have to. *The best way to combat shame is to face it.* I want to grab it by its throat and let it go but I know the only way I can do that is if I look at it first. I don't want to, but I know I have to.

you are here,
somewhere in between
his leaving and
your becoming.

somewhere in between

You are here,
somewhere in between his leaving and your becoming,
feeling dry, close to empty.
Imagine the earth cracked by the sun.
Imagine this as shelter—
an excuse to protect yourself.
There are hills and valleys and you are here,
somewhere in between.

I believe it to be a trauma thing, a very beautiful thing: the wanting, the doubting, the insecurity. Believe me, I know how heavy it all is.

Maybe you *are* safe. Maybe you *are* with a good person, in a good place. Maybe you have no reason to doubt who you are and what you're capable of. Sometimes, though, your mind just makes it up to be this way. This is what your soul is used to, what it expects.

I believe that insecurity is a means of warning, telling you that you are in need of healing.

If you are with someone who is right for you, they will remind you each and every day of your worth, your capabilities, and the things that make you stand out from the rest. They will never give you a reason to feel insecure. They will reassure you in however way you need them to.

And while it's important to be with someone who is good for your heart and soul, it's just as important to take time to learn about yourself and why you might be feeling the way you do.

Spend time alone. Figure out what growth feels like. Understand the way you love yourself and which parts of you need a little more tenderness.

hard pill to swallow

Let him go, I tell myself, every time I see him with her. I want him to be doing fine but not better than me and I'm not sure what that says about me other than maybe it's a petty thing. An ugly thing. A hard pill to swallow thing. A *Why couldn't he have loved me like that?* thing.

memory of a flame

Please, be patient. Every person who you believed was the one for you will bury themselves into a distilled memory the way they're supposed to. They will melt into the back of your mind the way ash does into wax after falling from a flame.

Wait for it.

change

It will hurt at first,
like watching glass shatter
and picking up the pieces
and not knowing where to put them
because you don't want to hurt anyone else.
I should tell you
how the things you keep close are easiest to break,
how sometimes the things we don't
want are inevitably ours
to experience,
how it will hurt like growing pains.

You don't have to be grateful for the trauma, my therapist tells me, and suddenly I see it all for what it really is—

I used to be grateful for the ones who didn't love me back, who left me aching, who led me to believe that what happened to me was a means of being a woman who loves harder and longer than I should. I believe everything happens for a reason, but what happened to me in love wasn't meant to. I believe that justifying pain is as harmful as being grateful for it.

Now, the hurt is demanding to be dealt with and looked at. Letting it be—after all this time—gave it power it didn't need.

I can be grateful for the art I create as a means of coping and healing from the pain I felt. I can be grateful for all the love I gave and the love I still give and the love that has found its way back to me. I can be grateful for the woman I became, with all my strength and love and hope, simply because that is who I am, not because it's who the pain forced me to grow into.

"you don't
have to
be grateful
for the trauma."

Let me be honest with you — there is nothing peaceful about your healing. In fact, your healing can be a very unbeautiful thing. But it is still very necessary. Your healing is necessary.

Let me be honest with you—there is nothing peaceful about your healing. In fact, your healing can be a very unbeautiful thing. It's loud and angry. It's terrifyingly lonely and quiet, too. But despite all these things, your healing is still important. Your healing is still necessary. Your healing is everything you hate, but that just means it's giving you the space to grow.

it will get easier

I should tell you it gets easier:
loving someone who doesn't love you back.
It will get easier—
if you say this enough times,
you will start to believe it.

I should tell you, it gets easier: loving someone who doesn't love you back.

It will get easier — if you say this enough times, you will start to believe it.

the end of it

Our lackluster togetherness was a joke and
I am wholeheartedly applauding at the end of it.

attraction

I know it hurts—more than you expected—
falling and losing yourself along the way,
but you have to believe that you are a force
and the laws of attraction are in your favor,
because, again, you are a force. You can take
one step and set the world on fire. You can
spark a flame if you believe it can happen.

liked it enough / bloomed

I never really loved my body
but I liked it enough
to feel okay looking in the mirror,
I liked it enough
to feel good wearing a floral sundress,
I liked it enough

until the doctor told me
my trauma had bloomed into a chronic pain
that would take time and energy and love
to heal.
Now, my body is in fight or flight.
I am tightening, caving in.

grieved

Between him and me,
it was only ever halfway, almost, not quite,
and I grieved the end of us
just the same.
I grieved as much as my heart would let me.

the healing body

He touches my stomach and all I can think about is bodywork, a healing practice for recovery, for undigested trauma. *The Body Keeps The Score* teaches the connection between the mind and body, how your brain can remember moments you want to forget and forget details you need to remember in order to heal. *Losing your body, losing yourself,* it tells me. I pray for a sense of peace, for a feeling of comfort in my own body being entwined with his. *Please.* How easy it is for everyone else, having these moments of intimacy, with mouths and tongues. *Please.* How often I beg for it.

the healing body

wanting/fearing

It is one of the most agonizing feelings in
the world, wanting intimacy but fearing it
just the same. Wanting to be close to some-
one and the moment it happens, it hurts.
My mind remembers and reminds my body
and there is nothing I can do about it.

soon

I know how hard it is
to be surrounded by all these bodies and faces and souls
and still feel completely lost and utterly alone.
I know what it is like
to stand in a rainstorm
and feel like you are drowning.
But please,
believe me
when I say this storm will pass.
Soon you will rise above it.
Soon it will be easier to breathe.

remember this

The healing will hurt until it doesn't anymore.

you are here, in this room

Close your eyes
and think of the living room as a metaphor.
You are here: your naked body,
wrapped in a bed sheet and curled up on a couch cushion.
In this quiet space, this full room,
you are here with the lint on the carpet
and the dust on the windowsill. I know it feels dirty
and the space feels more empty than anything else,
but I promise it isn't.
You are here, in this room,
where the walls are expanding
and the curtains are opening by themselves
so the light can peek in.
Can you see it?

remember —

recovery is
far from easy,
but each day is
a moment of
healing.

the part of trauma no one talks about

No one really talks about how hard it is to navigate intimacy when you have trauma sitting heavy on your chest like the devil on your shoulder. No one really talks about that agony of thinking about sex as being both a heavy burden and a means of coping.

Some days you will find yourself breaking down into full sobs—body shaking, face aching, tears streaming down your face. If you are here, let it happen. Some days it will be dark and you will find it difficult to get out of bed. Sometimes you might force yourself to get close to another person just so you can feel something good again, something different, something like euphoria.

You will learn what it means to be kind to your body but to still push yourself out of your comfort zone. You will learn how to forgive yourself for how often you cry, to let yourself feel what you feel. You will learn to feel comfortable in your body with someone else's. Although, right now, you feel like your trauma has power over you, you are braver and stronger because of this.

Remember: recovery is far from easy, but each day is a moment of healing.

this is me trying

This is me trying to understand the mind/body connection / how I'm never in the mood because of the antidepressants I've been taking for years / how I've been taking the antidepressants because my anxiety is ugly and the man who is assaulted me is uglier and thinking about both of those things is exhausting.

This is me trying to understand why I can't have sex / or if I'll ever have sex again / why I can't make love to the person I love even though I know I'm safe with him / why trauma has to hurt this bad / why the physical pain executes from the mental pain / and the repressed memories / why I can't just forget it ever happened.

This is me trying to understand that it's okay to cry every time I think about intimacy / when I try to be intimate. / I think this is a means of healing. I think this is me trying to get better.

this is me
trying to
get better.

we'll be alright

When you finally let go of the person you loved, who had trouble loving you just the same, it will hurt like a growing pain. The fact of the matter is that healing is supposed to hurt. It's your heart's way of telling you, *We're getting better. We'll be alright.*

believe it

*I no longer weigh myself down with a 'him.' I
no longer measure the distance between us.*

The more you tell yourself this, the
more you will start to believe it.

You pick the petals off one by one—*he loves me, he loves me not*—and wonder if you'll ever have those good feelings again: the giddiness of catching them looking at you, the calmness of being close, the vulnerability, the intimacy of holding hands.

Listen, the longing and the mourning will eat you alive if you let it. So please, don't let it get to you. Let yourself bloom in place of what was lost.

Think of him as someone who no longer gets to be loved by you. Hold the memories of him in the palm of your hand like a piece of forbidden, rotten fruit.

Remind yourself that just because he left doesn't mean you're any less lovable or that someone new won't come along and treat you the way you deserve and give you those good feelings again.

Remind yourself that just because he left doesn't mean you're any less lovable or that someone new won't come along and treat you the way you deserve and give you those good feelings again.

easy to forget

I kiss the boys
and mold their bodies
until they start to take shape in my mind
or until they become invisible.
Every inch of them is etched in my memory:
the curved spines, the freckles cheeks, the rippled palms.
Slowly,
they melt into something.
They are easy to forget.

feelings of acceptance

I am learning what it means
to let go of the ones I have loved
a little too hard
and for a little too long.
How exhausting it all was.
How sad I felt,
coming to terms with what's happening between us.
How lonely I felt when I was drowning in it all.

dreaming, uprooting

My therapist tells me that seeing old lovers in my dreams is a sign of healing, a means of facing the undigested: the desire I had to be significant to them, the sad belief that our togetherness shouldn't have had an expiration date, the way I blossomed into a woman with them, in the moments we shared. In these dreams, I am subconsciously uprooting the old trauma, even after I worked so hard to bury it. Seeing their faces in my mind is more than just missing them, but letting them go, in a way I didn't think I needed to. I'm not sure what it all means other than it being something I will have to live with until I don't need to anymore.

I am subconsciously
uprooting old trauma,

even after I worked
so hard to bury it.

I wonder why we're
so quick to love others,
why we forget to give
some of that love to
ourselves, especially when
we are the ones who
need it the most.

I wonder why we are so quick to love others,
why we forget to give some of that love to ourselves,
especially when we're the ones who need it the most.

When you love someone, it can be hard to move on. But one day it will get easier. Every thought, every feeling, every memory will grow distant. And then you will start to heal.

It was not my fault / I will heal

There is something to be said about bravery, the strength to heal after it all happens, the wanting to find peace in your body with another's. Tell yourself this, over and over again, until it sinks in: *It was not my fault. I will heal.* Please, remember this. It was not your fault and you will heal.

I wonder what it is about certain
people and why we hold onto them,
even if we know they're no good for us.

When you love someone, you start to notice things: the way their fingers curl around yours and soften as they fall asleep next to you. How, when they smile, wrinkles form and crease around their eyes. The softness of their voice in the morning, how they hum and the world goes quiet.

Then, one day, you start to realize it—that maybe this is all there is. Maybe they are elusive. Maybe the space between you two is nothing more than just space.

I wonder what it is about certain people and why we hold onto them, even if we know they're no good for us. The ones who reassure us that we *are* wanted and needed, but not enough, not in the ways we want them to. The ones who embrace their inconsistency. The ones who remind us they don't actually believe in love and maybe, you shouldn't either.

Let me be the first to say that I know how hard it is to love someone and realize you should let them go. I know that feeling of disappointment—it sits heavy in the pit of you, unmoving. I know how hard it is to distance yourself from them because, in your heart, you believe in it. You believe in *something*. Fate, maybe. The right timing. Euphoria.

But no matter what fate has planned and no matter how much you love someone, if you start to doubt yourself and who you are and what you believe in, you have to let them go.

what's the use?

I know what you're thinking: *What's the use? It's hard to be hopeful when nothing looks hopeful.*

Even though you don't see something in the palm of your hands doesn't mean it's not at your fingertips. Maybe you're one of the lucky ones and you just don't see it yet. Maybe there's something to be said about patience.

maybe you're one of the
lucky ones and you
just don't see it yet.

maybe there's something
to be said about patience.

I knew I couldn't make you love me
but that doesn't mean it didn't hurt
any less when you didn't.

euphoric

There's a difference between sex therapy and using sex as a means of therapy, but whatever it is, I'm still learning how to heal. I'm still learning how to come to terms with the fact that crying after sex isn't the prettiest thing I've done, but that's okay, and letting someone in is a way of coping, and that's okay too. Last night I saw what it was like to come to clarity, to be face-to-face with my fear and stick my fingers in its mouth. *You're okay. You're safe.* Trauma is a heavy burden. *You're healing.*

hands are just hands

When you realize you've finally let go of that person who was no good for you, the sky will be pink. The air will feel different and you just might find yourself crying because of it. You will notice this feeling after it rains: when the gold of the sun and the silver of the rain wed and there is a subtle lightness to the air and everything is covered in dew.

It will all feel a bit strange at first, as if you should be longing for something or as if you've forgotten something but you can't remember what. And then suddenly, you will understand how this was inevitable: the meeting and the parting. How your togetherness never really felt like it was truly together, but hanging on by a thread.

When you realize you are peeling away memories of them like the skin of a clementine, the rainy days will feel less heavy and the dew on the flowers will look the way your favorite song feels.

When you start to let them go from your grip, you'll see that your body feels lighter. You'll come to understand that your parting is a good thing and each day will get easier. You'll look back on who you saw them as when you were together and when you were wearing rose-colored glasses, and you will realize that their laugh is anything but poetic and their hands are just hands.

when you realize you've finally let go of the person who was no good for you, the sky will be pink.

it will all feel a bit strange at first,

as if you should be longing for something but you can't remember what. and then suddenly, you will understand how this was inevitable: the meeting and the parting.

Sometimes you love someone who is no good for you. And sometimes you have to let yourself leave them before you lose yourself in them completely.

I want you to look at this as a good thing. Think of your parting as serendipitous because, without it, you wouldn't be where you are now.

Trust in that this was supposed to happen for you to feel open and at peace. The light will come in, but only if you let it.

after it ends

The first thing you will feel is grief.
You will find yourself in the breathing room,
where everything is quiet
and uncertainty feels as heavy as the door that let you in,
but you should stay here for a bit.
After it ends,
you will feel something different.
Relief, maybe.
Happiness—
eventually.

wilt

Be gentle with yourself—
your soft body and lonely arms.
Quiver, if you have to, but don't let him see.
Will he come back? Does he miss me too?
Don't think of that right now.
He doesn't matter anymore—what mat-
ters is how he made you feel
and how you can heal from it.
Loving him made you wither, can't you see that?
Take that grief and plant it somewhere else.

loving him made
you wither, can't
you see that?

take that
grief and
plant it
somewhere
else.

I always thought it was strange
you never knew just how much I loved you,
how badly I wanted you to love me the same way.
But what does it mean when you call me a year later,
a year after we ended things?
I think about everything I will nev-
er have the courage to ask,
Did you ever feel the same way?
Are you realizing now that maybe you did?

did you ever feel
the same
way?
are you
realizing
now that
maybe you
did?

a moment

Sometimes you will catch yourself doing it.
You will think of him,
even long after you have parted ways,
even if you both have moved on and
are looking at life differently.
Sometimes you will think of him
and you will wonder if he is thinking of you too.
You will start to believe
your time together was simply a moment in time,
a moment shared in this Universe,
between two souls who found one another
and let each other go
because they had to.

I wonder what it's like
to not feel something for someone,
even after it all ends.

the parting of

In all its glory,
the water kisses the sand
with heavy breathing
and it is like us, the same
enveloping of one another
in wetness and salt.
There is a visible softness
to the ripples, the stretch marks,
his hands on my thighs,
Parting.

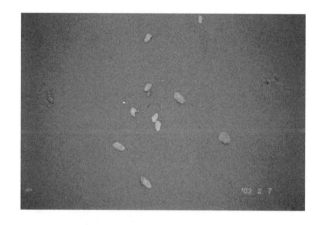

it is like us, the
same enveloping of
one another, in
wetness and salt.

a beautiful feeling

Tell me,
what's a more beautiful feeling:
realizing—
for the first time—
that you love someone,
or realizing
you've finally gotten over someone you used to love?

beautiful things

His hands / the warmth I feel inside of my body
when I think about his fingers on my skin / the
good / the transparency / the closeness / his neck
/ the sound of his laugh, bellowing from his chest
/ the lightness of his smile / how he invited me
into his little world with grace and ease / how I
invited him into my world just the same.

He calls you a year and a half after things end between you two and the sound of his voice plays on repeat in your mind like an old song you used to love. you listen to the way he says your name and you remember why it was your favorite sound. But please, don't sit with this for too long. Tell yourself this is just noise. He is just noise.

your favorite sound

He calls you a year and a half after things end between you two and the sound of his voice plays on repeat in your mind like an old song you used to love. You listen to the way he says your name and you remember why it was your favorite sound. But please, don't sit with this for too long. Tell yourself this is just noise. He is just noise.

When you're in love, it feels like the world is bigger. The sky becomes bluer and brighter. The sound of the wind blowing through the trees becomes something of a song and all that matters is the way they make you feel. You romanticize them and the moments you share with them. Everything becomes poetry. This person becomes something of substance in your mind. You believe in beautiful things because you believe this person is one of those things. You get lost in it.

It isn't until they leave you that you start to see things for what they were, and even then, it's not easy to see right away. At first, you feel your world shrinking. You convince yourself it was something you did or didn't do. It was your fault they left in the first place. And again, you get lost in that.

I know how hard it is to care for someone and still know they're not good for you. You wear the rose-colored glasses as if you're supposed to, and you let the rest be.

Let me tell you the truth: the kind of love that makes you fearful or anxious, or the love that runs away when things get difficult—that is not real love. The kind of love that is forbidden to the world and kept secret for reasons they won't explain and you will never understand—that is not real love.

When you're young and in love—or what you think is love—all you see is good. The fact of the matter is, not everyone you love will love you the same way. Whether it be lust or something greater, not everyone you let yourself be with will be good for you or good to you.

And sometimes, the love you want isn't the love you deserve.

If you're one of the lucky ones who found love to be something wild, hold onto that. If they leave you with the memories, keep them close, but bury them. Use them as a reason to keep going. Keep holding on for a love that feels full, one that shouldn't be romanticized or seen through rose-colored glasses. Forgive yourself. Wait for the love you deserve.

wait for the
love you deserve.

Just as dust settles into the nooks
and crannies of my pockets,
you will always hold a place in my heart.

hate or indifference

They say the opposite of love isn't hate,
but indifference.
When it comes to you,
I'm not sure how I feel.
Even after all this time,
even after all the hurt.

afterwards

Nobody really talks about what it's *really* like afterwards:
how healing is more like *trying* to heal;
how sex is looked at as a burden,
something a little too unbearable;
how tired you will feel
every time you try to have sex with someone you love
because you want it to happen for you,
so you push yourself.
But then it hurts,
and you're in his bedroom when the panic starts
with his fingers tucking strands of hair behind your ear
because he knows it eases anxiety.
I want someone to talk about this.
I need to know I'm not as weak as I think I am.

I'm not sure which is worse:
him loving her or him not loving me.

I find myself thinking about all the loves I've had in this life—the ones I had to let go of in order to grow, the ones who held me back from growing, the ones who broke me in ways I didn't think was possible, the ones who spent more time ruining me than loving me.

I think of the one with the laugh and how badly I wish I could hear it now, especially on the days I need some light. I daydream about the one who I talked for hours with about the new book he's reading or some of my favorite songs. I wonder about the one with the addictions, if he's doing okay now and if he's thinking of me too.

I look back on all the small moments I shared with him: the softness to his eyes looking at me in the morning, the way he would stretch his limbs out to kiss me *good morning*. I think about the coffee he made me and the bottles of wine we shared, the movies we used to watch together, the songs we used to sing together in the shower.

When I find myself thinking about the old loves I've had in this life, I let myself feel whatever it is I feel. I don't push away the thoughts of them because I know it's okay to think about them from time to time.

They were someone important to me at one point in this life, someone who I once shared beautiful moments with, someone who made me who I am today—and that is something to be grateful for.

I fell in love
with myself
when I fell out of love
with him.

fell in / fell out

I fell in love with myself when I fell out of love with him. I watched him lose me for good and my eyes glazed over. Now, I notice the morning dew, and I eat this moment up.

If you, too, find yourself thinking about the loves you've had, try not to get lost in that thinking, especially the what-ifs. It's okay to miss them. It's okay to miss what you shared with them.

Whatever you're thinking of—just don't let it consume you. Don't let these thoughts take control of your feelings. Don't second guess where you are now or who you're with or if you made the right decision.

Think of these loves as people who you were meant to know and love at one point in time, but that's it. They are in the past for a reason. Remember that.

strength

I believe it to be some kind of ethereal strength,
having enough courage
to tell someone you love them when you do,
especially when you know they don't love you
in the same way.

divine timing

It's funny, isn't it?
How the Universe moves along
and creates magic
in her own divine timing.
And how easy it was for her to
bring us together as if we were supposed to.
They say you attract what you expect,
and when you meet a soulmate, you'll know.

magic

I believe there is magic in loving,
but I also believe that
only the right people deserve that
kind of love you have to give.

something I'm learning about love—

There are some people in your life that you can't help but love so fiercely, no matter what. Sometimes, these people don't love you the same, or at all, and that is okay. Not everyone you love will love you in return, and while that might make you want to shrink, please do not let it harden you too.

The love you gave to them—and will continue to give to others—is the most beautiful thing about you. People like you—people who love hard and good—don't come easy in this life. It takes a lot for some people to do what you do so easily and with so much courage and conviction.

If you happen to love someone who could not match your capacity to love, remind yourself that's okay. You have left them with a light that is so bright and so rare. You left them with the memories of a courageous soul, the kind that comes few and far between. Whether or not they know it and will admit it, you were a great person to them. They were lucky to have known you and be loved by you.

And now, you are able to walk away and meet someone who can and will love you in the same way and in the way you deserve to be loved. So please, do not hold yourself back, clinging onto a person not meant for you. Remind yourself of the power you hold. Wait for a love that is right and good.

it's in these
little wonders
that I almost lost
all faith in.

little wonders

They say you should tell people how you feel about them
before it's too late
but I think time is on our side,
or maybe the Universe is showing us
what it means to pray for something,
even if we are going in blindly, as nonbelievers do.
Maybe that is why we feel the way we do.
The sky opens and we float.
Do you believe in heaven?
It's in these little wonders that I start
to believe in something
I almost lost all faith in.

he is a poem

Trying to write a poem about the person you love is hard, even when you're a poet, even when there's so much you want to say but don't know how to put into words. He is a poem. I don't even have to say anything else.

heaven

I can't stop thinking about it—the freckles on his spine, how they look like a cluster of stars; how my mom used to tell me that freckles are kisses from angels; how I don't think I believe in Heaven but that maybe there's something to be said about the way I feel when I'm with him.

when you meet a soulmate, you will feel it

I can't help but think there's a deeper meaning to it—
that fluttering nervousness in the pit of your stomach.
The butterflies feel like a metaphor for something unset-
tling, an omen. Something you don't even have a name
for. A gut instinct: *they're not the one and that's okay.*

The butterflies-in-your-stomach-feeling is your soul's
way of showing you that maybe they aren't your person.
Or maybe, they were someone important to you in an-
other life or in another Universe and that's why you feel
the way you do now. It's your soul's way of telling you
that this person is someone to notice.

When you meet a soulmate, you will feel it. You will feel
calm, like reuniting with an old friend. In your gut, it will
feel as if you've crossed time and space to meet again.
You will see the butterflies dancing around your head,
celebrating the reunion. You will feel your insides getting
warm. When you meet the person who *is* meant for you,
your body will tell you the only way it knows how.

lullaby

Your laugh echoes in my chest like a
lullaby I never want to forget.

lucky

He writes a song about the new girl he loves
and all I can think about is the way he used to play me,
fingering my spine like a guitar,
taking notes from the whirring fan's song.
How lucky she must feel
to hear him sing her to sleep every night,
how lucky she must be
to know the little white lines aren't blurring his thinking
or melting his voice
like how when he was with me.
How lucky she is—
he doesn't have to convince her that he loves her.

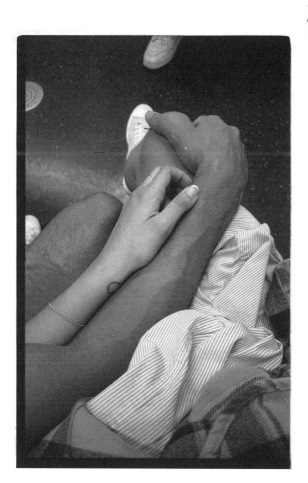

Love is something I never thought I'd have a name for, but I see it now, and it's him.

It was ugly, the first time I had a panic attack in front of him.

The lamplight on the bedside table was dimmed but he could still see my face, wet and sad. It was cold in the room but we had each others' body heat and that was all that mattered to us. He held me close and silently, wiping my face with his bare hands.

I don't like people seeing me cry. I don't like showing that I have been hurt or that I am hurting. I'm normally a very vulnerable, open person, but something about crying feels different. I mean, I know crying isn't a sign of weakness but I still feel that way. It's like if I try to peel myself out of bed, I won't make it very far.

But that night, as ugly as it all was, he was still kind. Gentle. Understanding. I didn't even realize how in love with him I was until that moment.

I understand it all now, how love is about those ugly moments.

Love is showing them who you are and what you look like when you're feeling weak with the weight of trauma or feeling confused and frustrated and angry, not knowing how to let it all go. Love is not understanding an anxiety disorder and antidepressants and the heavy burden of trauma, but holding your hand through it all anyway.

Love is holding someone when they cry and using your bare hands as tissues. Love is letting the person sob, no matter how heavy or quiet. Love is not having the right words to say in those dark moments except *Let it out. I'm here.*

Love is something I never thought I'd have a name or a face for, but I see it now, and it's him.

I like to think that maybe
being in our own little corner
of the universe is where we're
meant to be,

like our meeting is inevitable
and in every parallel reality,
we are supposed to end up
together.

in every parallel reality

I like to think that maybe being in our own little corner of the Universe is where we're meant to be, like our meeting is inevitable and in every parallel reality, we are supposed to end up together.

love stories

Sometimes we find ourselves writing love stories and convincing ourselves it's the Universe's doing. And maybe it is. Maybe some love stories with certain souls *are* in the hands of the Universe. But maybe there are some love stories that are not necessarily meant to be. We write those kinds of stories together, or alone. We write stories about loving someone who does not love us back. We write stories about how we are learning to love after loss. Whether it's written in the stars or something you're writing by yourself or with someone else, the love you will experience in this life is more significant than you ever can imagine.

a poem about self-love, for once

I have always watched the lovers come and go
like a revolving door,
but with each passing day,
I see it all differently:
how soft I am,
how I romanticize moments
and people
and moments I share with those people,
how hard I love,
even for those who don't deserve it.
I see it all differently now,
how this is about me.
How I fill a room
with light,
body heat,
and the kind of love people write songs about.

delicate

The way he loves me is delicate,
as if I am a disco ball
twirling in a sunlit room.

the way he loves
me is delicate,

as if I am a
discoball twirling
in a sunlit room.

looking for love

The love that is meant to be yours will find you
when you stop looking for it.
And when it comes, it will make itself known
and you'll think,
oh, it's you I was looking for,
and you'll understand that
things come together when they're supposed to.
So when love comes, open your heart.
Watch it fit and fold together
the way it was meant to.

The first time he told me he loved me, I was in the kitchen peeling sweet potatoes. It felt like such a mundane, yet marvelous, moment to tell me this, but he did it anyway and it was the most beautiful feeling I've ever felt in return.

I believe that love is about the quiet moments. To love and to be loved in return—sometimes, that can be quite simple. The thing is, telling someone that you love them doesn't always have to be this extraordinary thing. It doesn't always have to be grand gestures and big moments that make the heart flutter. A *this-is-what-I've-been-waiting-for* kind of moment.

It's the shivers down my spine when I feel his fingers tucking strands of hair behind my ear because he knows it eases my anxiety. It's falling asleep together and realizing our bodies have separated in the night, but we are still holding hands anyway.

It's the way he looks at me while I read, the feeling I get in my chest *knowing* he's looking at me while I read, and smiling. It's being close in a small kitchen, making dinner, and singing whatever song was stuck in our heads that day. Love doesn't always have to be a shout-from-the-rooftops kind of passion. Sometimes love is simple. It's just a quiet moment of feeling.

Sometimes love is simple.
It's just a quiet moment
of feeling.

KELLY PEACOCK is a writer living in NYC.

instagram.com/kellyapeacock

MORE FROM
THOUGHT CATALOG BOOKS

A Gentle Reminder
—*Bianca Sparacino*

Ceremony
—*Brianna Wiest*

Everything You'll Ever Need
(You Can Find Within Yourself)
—*Charlotte Freeman*

Beyond Worthy
—*Jacqueline Whitney*

**THOUGHT
CATALOG**
Books

THOUGHTCATALOG.COM
NEW YORK · LOS ANGELES